Be My Galentine

ST. MARTIN'S GRIFFIN ≈ NEW YORK

Be My Galentine

Celebrating Badass Female Friendship

ALICIA CLANCY

ILLUSTRATED BY SAMANTHA FARRAR

www.stmartins.com

Illustrations by Samantha Farrar

The Library of Congress Cataloging-in-Publication Data is available upon request.

ISBN 978-1-250-13085-3 (paper over board)
ISBN 978-1-250-13086-0 (e-book)

Our books may be purchased in bulk for promotional, educational, or business use. Please contact your local bookseller or the Macmillan Corporate and Premium Sales Department at 1-800-221-7945, extension 5442, or by e-mail at MacmillanSpecialMarkets@macmillan.com.

First Edition: January 2017

10 9 8 7 6 5 4 3 2 1

TO MY GALENTINE

FRIENDS WHO PEE TOGETHER
STAY TOGETHER.

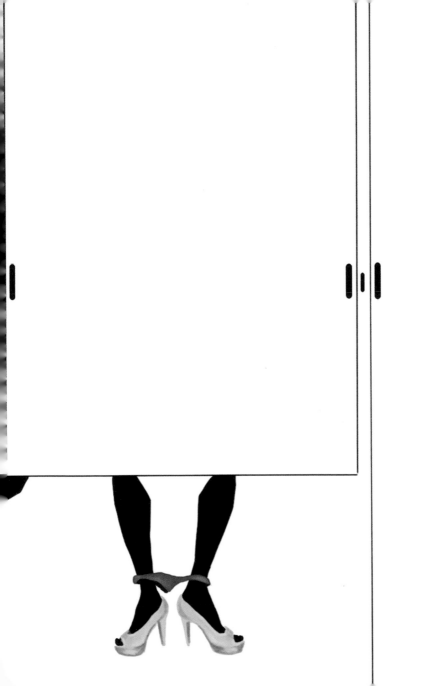

Gal pals don't care if your apartment is messy. They only care if you have wine.

THANKS FOR SWIDING LEFT ON
ALL THOSE TINDER GUYS MY
THIRD GLASS OF WINE TOLD
ME TO SWIDE RIGHT ON.

Thanks for teaching me the rule of association: We re hungry. Swimsuit models hungry. Therefore, we are swimsuit models.

THANKS FOR BEING ONE
OF THOSE PEOPLE I WANT TO
DRINK WITH RATHER THAN ONE
OF THOSE PEOPLE WHO
MAKES ME WANT TO DRINK.

WINTER SANGRIA

White Cranberry Sangria

2 bottles pinot grigio
1/4 cup sugar
1 cup fresh cranberries
1 cup diced red apples
sprig of rosemary
2 cups sparkling apple cider

1 In a large bowl, combine the wine and sugar and stir until the sugar dissolves.

2 Add the cranberries, apples, and rosemary and refrigerate until well chilled, about 1 hour.

3 Remove from the refrigerator and add the sparkling apple cider. Serve in glasses over ice.

Pomegranate-Cinnamon Sangria

2 bottles red wine
1/4 cup brandy
1/4 cup sugar
1/2 cup pomegranate seeds
1 pear, diced
cinnamon stick
2 cups Sprite

1 In a large bowl, combine the wine, brandy, and sugar and stir until the sugar dissolves.

2 Add the pomegranate seeds, pear, and cinnamon and refrigerate until well chilled, about 1 hour.

3 Remove from the refrigerator and add the Sprite. Serve in glasses over ice.

SPRING SANGRIA

Rose Petal Sangria
2 bottles rosé
1/4 cup elderflower cordial
1/4 cup rose petal simple syrup
1/4 cup sugar
food-grade fresh rose petals soaked in lemon water
mint leaves
2 cups Sprite

1. In a large bowl, combine the wine, cordial, simple syrup, and sugar and stir until the sugar dissolves.
2. Refrigerate until well chilled, about 1 hour.
3. Remove from the refrigerator, stir in the rose petals and mint leaves, and add the Sprite. Serve in glasses over ice.

Berry Spring Sangria

2 bottles zinfandel
1/2 cup gin
splash of orange juice
1/4 cup sugar
1 cup diced strawberries
1 cup blackberries
1 orange, thinly sliced
2 cups ginger ale

1 In a large bowl, combine the wine, gin, orange juice, and sugar and stir until the sugar dissolves.

2 Add the strawberries, blackberries, and orange slices and refrigerate until well chilled, about 1 hour.

3 Remove from the refrigerator and add the ginger ale. Serve in glasses over ice.

SUMMER SANGRIA

Strawberry Peach Bliss

1 bottle pinot grigio
1/4 cup sugar
1 cup diced strawberries
1/2 cup diced red apples
1/2 cup diced peaches
1 bottle sparkling peach wine
2 cups Sprite

1. In a large bowl, combine the wine and sugar and stir until the sugar dissolves.
2. Add the strawberries, apples, and peaches and refrigerate until well chilled, about 1 hour.
3. Remove from the refrigerator and add the sparkling wine and the Sprite. Serve in glasses over ice.

Frosty Summer Sangria

2 bottles cabernet sauvignon, well chilled
1/4 cup sugar
1 peeled orange, segmented
1 peeled lemon, segmented
1 pound frozen mixed berries
2 cups ginger ale
whole small strawberries or strawberry slices

1. In a large bowl, combine the wine and sugar and stir until the sugar dissolves.
2. Add to a blender the wine-sugar mixture, orange, lemon, and frozen berries. Blend well until combined to a smoothie-like consistency. Pour into a pitcher and stir in the ginger ale.
3. Pour into glasses and garnish with a whole strawberry or strawberry slices.

FALL SANGRIA

Caramel Apple Sangria

2 bottles moscato
1/4 cup caramel vodka
2 Red Delicious apples, diced
cinnamon stick
2 cups sparkling apple cider

1 In a large bowl, combine the wine and vodka.

2 Add the apples and cinnamon stick and refrigerate until well chilled, about 1 hour.

3 Remove from the refrigerator and add the sparkling apple cider. Serve in glasses over ice.

Honeycrisp Apple Sangria

1 bottle cabernet sauvignon
1/4 cup apple brandy
2 tablespoons honey
2 Honeycrisp apples, diced
1/2 cup pomegranate seeds
1 bottle prosecco

1. In a large bowl, combine the wine, brandy, and honey and stir until the sugar dissolves.
2. Add the apples and pomegranate seeds and refrigerate until well chilled, about 1 hour.
3. Remove from the refrigerator and add the prosecco. Serve in glasses over ice.

A true galentine knows the best way to your heart.

REAL BESTIES WILL ALWAYS
FORGIVE YOUR ECCENTRICITIES.

Thanks for pausing your own Snapchat Story long enough to watch mine. That's friendship.

A GOOD FRIEND BUYS
YOU FOOD. A BEST FRIEND
SAYS SHE'S NOT HUNGRY
AND THEN PROCEEDS TO
EAT ALL OF YOUR FOOD.

Caprese Bites

cherry tomatoes
1 ball fresh mozzarella
fresh basil leaves
organic olive oil

1 Slice each cherry tomato in half.
2 On bottom halves, add a small slice of fresh mozzarella and a fresh basil leaf, then drizzle lightly with olive oil.
3 Place top half of tomato back on top, and use a toothpick to hold together if needed. Enjoy!

Frozen Greek Yogurt Pomegranate Bites

2 cups vanilla Greek yogurt
1/2 cup powdered sugar (optional)
2/3 cup pomegranate seeds

1 Whisk yogurt, powdered sugar, and pomegranate seeds together.
2 Using either large ice-cube trays or a mini muffin pan, scoop mixture into mold, then freeze for 3–4 hours until solid.
3 You can also substitute strawberries or blueberries if you prefer. Enjoy!

Goat Cheese-and-Honey Poppers

log of goat cheese
2/3 cup flour
pinch of salt and pepper
1/2 cup bread crumbs
1 egg, beaten
cooking oil, any type
2 tablespoons honey

1. Cut the goat cheese into bite-size pieces and roll into balls.
2. Mix flour, salt, pepper, and bread crumbs in a bowl.
3. Dip cheese balls first in the egg, then in the bread crumb mixture.
4. Heat a layer of oil in a deep skillet or fryer to 350 degrees Fahrenheit. Fry coated cheese balls until crispy all over. Remove from oil using a slotted spoon and let excess oil drain on paper towels.
5. Lightly drizzle with honey and serve. Enjoy!

Truffle Popcorn

1/3 cup organic popcorn kernels
2 tablespoons black truffle oil
pinch of truffle salt or pink Himalayan salt
1 tablespoon butter

1 Pour popcorn kernels into a metal pot. Add the black truffle oil until the kernels are just covered.

2 Cover the pot with a lid, set stove on medium-high heat, and wait for the popping to end.

3 Pour the popped kernels into a bowl and add the butter to the empty, still hot pot.

4 Once the butter has melted, pour over the kernels. Toss to coat, salt to taste, and enjoy!

Nutella Puffs

2 cups puffed quinoa or puffed rice cereal
1 cup Nutella
(peanut butter, cookie butter, and other spreads
with a similar consistency also work wonderfully)
1/4 stick melted butter
10-ounce bag of dark or milk chocolate chips

1 In a large bowl, combine puffs, melted butter, and
   Nutella.
2 Refrigerate the mixture for 10 minutes, then roll
   mixture into teaspoon-sized balls.
3 Melt the chocolate in a double boiler, then use the
   melted chocolate to coat the Nutella puffs.
4 Chill for one hour. Serve and enjoy!

A good friend brings over a bottle of wine to share. A <u>best</u> friend brings over two bottles.

TRUE GALENTINES HATE
WHEN ANYONE ELSE REFERS
TO <u>YOUR</u> BESTIE AS <u>THEIR</u>
BESTIE. THERE CAN ONLY BE
ONE, AND YOU ARE IT.

A best friend will never make fun of you for knowing all the words. Unless it's Nickelback, in which case you deserve to be made fun of.

'90s Throwback Playlist

Here's a great '90s–early 2000s pop playlist that is
perfect for slumber dance parties and road trips!

"Spice Up Your Life" by the Spice Girls

"Bye Bye Bye" by *NSYNC

"Barbie Girl" by Aqua

". . . Baby One More Time" by Britney Spears

"C'est La Vie" by B*Witched

"S Club Party" by S Club 7

"Playas Gon' Play" by 3LW

"Genie in a Bottle" by Christina Aguilera

"Candy" by Mandy Moore

"Say My Name" by Destiny's Child

"He Loves U Not" by Dream

"No Scrubs" by TLC

"Thong Song" by Sisqó

"It Wasn't Me" by Shaggy

"Hot in Herre" by Nelly

"I Want It That Way" by The Backstreet Boys

"MMMBop" by Hanson

"Love Don't Cost a Thing" by Jennifer Lopez

"Beautiful Soul" by Jesse McCartney

"The Boy Is Mine" by Brandy and Monica

"Cruel Summer" by Ace of Base

"Lady Marmalade" by Christina Aguilera,
Lil' Kim, Mya, and Pink

A TRUE GALENTINE IS ALWAYS WILLING TO STALK YOUR EX ON SOCIAL MEDIA WHEN YOU REGRET THE RASH DECISION YOU MADE TO BLOCK THEM.

What's up?

OMG!!!!!!!!!!!!!

Real besties have their
own language.

GALENTINES SHARE
EVERYTHING . . .

EXCEPT SHOES.
SHOES ARE SACRED.

Sleepover: Craft Edition

While it's fine to have a normal sleepover, it can also be a lot of fun to give the night a theme. For the creative gal pals, crafting can make for the perfect night! Of course, there are many crafts you could choose, but here are a few ideas to get you started in planning your very own crafting sleepover.

naughty cross-stitching

candle making

DIY glitter mason jars (these make fabulous vases)

wood burning

stenciling

paper crafts using books

stone painting

making hanging terrariums

pottery night at a BYOB studio

BYOB wine and painting classes at your local bar

making clay magnets

decorating fancy cupcakes

adult coloring books

water-gun painting

Sharpie mugs

bedazzled or glitter wineglasses

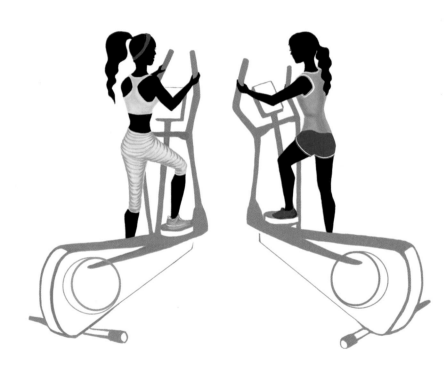

Thanks for warning me when someone cute is about to walk in at the gym, so I can pretend to be working out hard while making it look effortless.

BESTIES WILL ALWAYS
FAKE AN EMERGENCY TO
HELD YOU GET OUT OF
AN AWKWARD DATE.

Galentines are always
there for you when you have
"nothing to wear."

REAL BESTIES KNOW
WHICH ONE OF YOUR
BOOBS IS BIGGER.

What to Wear

Pub Golf is an opportunity to dress to a TEE.
Hehe, golf humor. But seriously, go all out!
Polo shirts, plaid and argyle, visor caps! If you
see it on the golf course, it's fair game! And, of
course, a golf glove is a MUST!

How It Works

Create scorecards (see example provided).
Each bar represents a hole. Each hole has an
associated drink and a par number.

So, for example, if you are at a bar with a par
one, that's a shot! If you have a par five, you
have five sips to finish the drink.

For any amount of sips over par, you must add
that to your score. The person with the highest
score at the end must chug a drink.

To make it even more interesting, bring a golf
ball. If you manage to get the golf ball into
someone's beverage, they must drink the
remainder of their beverage in one go!

NAME				
HOLE	BAR NAME	TYPE OF DRINK	PAR	SCORE
1	Bar One	beer or cider	3	
2	Bar Two	shot of tequila	1	
3	Bar Three	Redheaded Slut	2	
4	Bar Four	beer or cider	5	
5	Bar Five	Lemon Drop	1	
6	Bar Six	vodka + mixer	2	
7	Bar Seven	Martini	3	
8	Bar Eight	beer or cider	4	
9	Bar Nine	shot of your choice	1	
FINAL SCORE One heck of a night!				

Cocktail-Themed Bar Crawl

If you want to have a night out that's a little different from the norm, try a themed bar crawl with costumes. And what better theme for a bar crawl than . . . *cocktails*?!

Here's how it works:

You and your besties each choose a drink and dress appropriately. For example:

Dress as a devil and order an El Diablo.
Dress in derby clothing and order a Mint Julep.
Dress as a leprechaun and order a Guinness.
Dress as a zombie and order a Zombie.
Dress as a mermaid and order a Sea Breeze.
Dress as Rizzo from *Grease* and order a Pink Lady.
Dress in business attire and order a Manhattan.
Dress like Eve and order a Snakebite.
Dress like a Bond girl and order a Vesper.
Dress in floral and a lei and order a Blue Hawaiian.
Dress in vintage clothing and order an Old Fashioned.

Use your imagination!

Cheers to always having a
Thirsty Thursday date.

REAL GALENTINES
TEXT EVERY TINY DETAIL
OF THEIR DAY.

True friendship is when typically negative words become terms of endearment.

BESTIES TREAT YOUR FUR
BABIES LIKE THEIR OWN.

When you think of a girls' night in, what image comes to mind? Maybe running around with green face masks and cucumber slices over your eyes? Face masks are a lot of fun for sleepover nights and really easy to make with ingredients you probably have in your kitchen already. Here are a couple of facial mask recipes, all with a honey theme (natural acne fighter) for you and your girlfriends to try out!

Banana and Honey Mask

one medium-size banana
1 1/2 tablespoons raw honey
3 tablespoons plain yogurt

1 Mash the banana into a paste-like consistency. Add in the honey and yogurt and stir until well blended.

2 Begin by washing your face to prep for the mask. Apply mask to face and neck and let sit for 15–20 minutes. Rinse off with cold water.

Oatmeal and Honey Mask

1/3 cup ground oatmeal
1/2 cup hot water
1 tablespoon raw honey
3 tablespoons plain yogurt
1 egg white

1. Mix the oatmeal with the hot water. Once soft, add in the honey, yogurt, and egg white. Stir until all ingredients are well blended.
2. Begin by washing your face to prep for the mask. Apply mask to face and neck and let sit for 10–20 minutes. Rinse off with warm water.

Lemon and Honey Mask

1/2 lemon
1 1/2 tablespoons raw honey

1. Squeeze the lemon into a bowl. Add in the raw honey, then stir until ingredients are well blended.
2. Begin by washing your face to prep for the mask. Apply mask to face and neck and let sit for 15–30 minutes. Rinse off with cold water.

Avocado and Honey Mask

1/2 avocado
1 tablespoon raw honey
2 tablespoons hot water

1. Mash the avocado into a paste. Dissolve the honey in the hot water, then add it to the avocado. Stir all the ingredients together until well blended.
2. Begin by washing your face to prep for the mask. Apply mask to face and neck and let sit for 10 minutes. Rinse off with warm water.

Yogurt and Honey Mask

1 tablespoon plain yogurt
1 tablespoon honey
1 dash of cinnamon

1. Squeeze the lemon into a bowl. Add in the raw honey, then stir until ingredients are well blended.
2. Begin by washing your face to prep for the mask. Apply mask to face and neck and let sit for 15–30 minutes. Rinse off with cold water.

True galentines don't judge . . .
even when you order dessert
for dinner. Then join in.

BEST FRIENDS ARE ALWAYS THERE FOR YOU WHEN YOU NEED THEM. UNLESS IT'S THE SEASON FINALE OF <u>THE BACHELOR</u>. IN THAT CASE, YOU ARE ON YOUR OWN.

Bye
Felicia

Besties will always
let you know when you need
a little grooming. The truth
hurts sometimes.

THANKS FOR SUPPORTING
MY DECISION TO PURSUE
RETAIL THERAPY INSTEAD
OF ACTUAL THERAPY.

Bohemian Picnic Girls' Date

If you are looking for a fun daytime get-together, then look no further! Here are a few tips for how to have the perfect bohemian-themed picnic! This can be held indoors or outdoors.

Apparel

Think loose, flowy fabrics, florals, and lace! Maxi dresses and playsuits are ideal, and oversize sunglasses are a must!

Accessorize with flower crowns, head chains, and/or metallic flash tats! And don't be afraid to go barefoot!

Décor

Find a long, low communal table (or just a pretty table runner if a table is not easily transportable and you choose to host in a park or backyard). Decorate the table or runner with fresh flowers and green plants!

Surround table or runner with an assortment of pillows for seating. These don't need to match and actually look better if they don't!

Food

Finger foods work best for this arrangement. Here are a few suggestions:

fresh loaves of bread
a cheese plate
bowls of marinated olives and pickles
fresh-cut vegetables (carrots, peppers, and cucumbers work well) with hummus
bunches of grapes
finger sandwiches (chicken Waldorf salad is a great summer option!)
a variety of nuts and dried fruits
individual fruit tarts or cookies for dessert
and, of course, lots of wine or sangria!

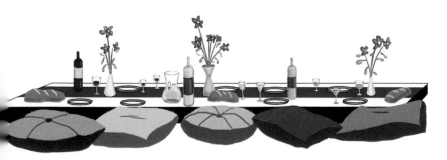

Besties cuddle.
Then just do.

TRUE FRIENDSHIP IS
COMING OUT OF A MEETING
TO FORTY-SEVEN MISSED TEXT
MESSAGES AND ONLY BEING
SLIGHTLY ANNOYED.

Thanks for pretending the new girlfriend is ugly even though we both know she isn't.

GALENTINES ARE ALWAYS
DOWN TO FAKE A LEG
CRAMP TO GET OUT
OF SPIN CLASS EARLY.

CHEEKY COCKTAILS

Cocktails with naughty names are just naturally more fun to drink! Here are a couple of recipes (single serving) for drinks with dirty names that are sure to take your pregame to the next level.

Sex with an Alligator

1/2 ounce melon liqueur
splash of sweet-and-sour mix
1/2 ounce raspberry liqueur
1/2 ounce Jägermeister

1. Add the melon liqueur and the sweet-and-sour mix to a shaker full of ice and shake until chilled.
2. Strain into a martini glass. Then add the raspberry liqueur by pouring down the side of the glass, allowing it to sink to the bottom.
3. Finish off by floating the Jägermeister, which will create a thin layer on top.
4. Insert cocktail straws and drink the whole glass in one go through the straws!

Redheaded Slut

1 ounce cranberry juice

1/2 ounce peach schnapps

1/2 ounce Jägermeister

1. Add all ingredients to a shaker full of ice and shake until chilled.
2. Strain into a shot glass for a fruity red shot.
3. Bottoms up!

Sex on the Beach

1 1/2 ounces vodka

1/2 ounce peach schnapps

1 1/2 ounces cranberry juice

1 1/2 ounces orange juice

orange wedge

1. Add all ingredients to a shaker full of ice and shake until chilled.
2. Strain into a highball glass.
3. Garnish with an orange wedge. Add a straw, sip, and enjoy!

TRUE FRIENDSHIP IS HAVING
BEEN FRIENDS SO LONG YOU
FORGET WHICH ONE OF
YOU IS THE BAD INFLUENCE.

A real galentine will always pretend to find <u>the friend</u> interesting long enough for you to get <u>the cute one's</u> number.

BESTIES WILL ALWAYS ROCK
OUT BESIDE YOU AT YOUR
FAVORITE BAND'S CONCERT,
EVEN IF THEY'VE NEVER
HEARD OF THEM BEFORE.

Galentines don't let galentines buy boxed wine. Unless they are broke. In which case, boxed wine > no wine.

Mimosa Bar

Brunch. Literally the best meal ever. You can get breakfast food or lunch food, and don't forget the mimosas! A fun (and less expensive) take on a brunch date is to host your own! Have everyone bring a food ingredient to cook, and, as the host, set up a mimosa bar for your gal pals to enjoy! Here's how to do it:

1. Start with chilled champagne or prosecco! Grab a few bottles depending on how many guests you invite.
2. Make sure you have enough flutes for everyone. You can always get disposable flutes at your local party store!
3. Have 3–5 juice options. Of course, the classic orange juice is a must-have! Mango juice, pomegranate juice, papaya juice, and strawberry juice are also delicious! Use your imagination!
4. Provide bowls of fresh fruit options: oranges, strawberries, pomegranate seeds, and diced peaches are just a few options that work nicely in mimosas.

It's as simple as that! Now all your friends can choose their own mimosa combination, and your brunch bash is sure to be a hit!

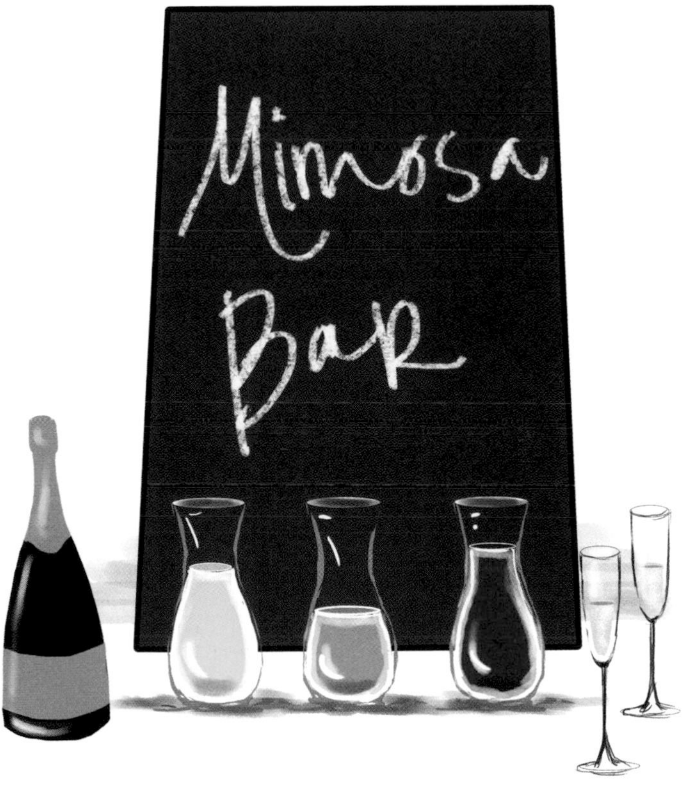
Mimosa Bar

Thanks for always suggesting fro-yo when I say "let's eat healthy."

BESTIES ARE ALWAYS THERE TO TALK YOU DOWN FROM YOUR WEBMD SPIRAL WHEN YOU'VE SELF-DIAGNOSED. YOU DO <u>NOT</u> HAVE DENGUE FEVER. YOU JUST DON'T.

True galentines are friends forever. And not only because they know all your secrets and could destroy you.

You
Feisty
Fiesta
Burrito

GAL PALS GIVE <u>EVERYTHING</u> THE WEIRDEST NICKNAMES. <u>ESPECIALLY EACH OTHER.</u>

Top 10 Things to Bring to a Girls'-Night-In Party

1. wine
2. any film starring Hugh Grant
3. nail polish
4. wine
5. chocolate anything
6. three types of cheese, minimum
7. wine
8. Skinny Pop (to give the illusion of healthiness)
9. Netflix subscription to binge-watch *Friends* and/or *Gilmore Girls*
10. and last but not least, WINE

Girls'-Night-In Movies

It's easy to get caught up watching the newest blockbuster features or Netflix series on your girls' night in. But, for those nights when you are feeling nostalgic, consider these classics that are sure to please!

Mean Girls
The Holiday
Love Actually
10 Things I Hate About You
How to Lose a Guy in 10 Days
Bridesmaids
27 Dresses
The Princess Diaries
13 Going on 30
any classic Disney film
Pretty Woman
Legally Blonde
Clueless
Bridget Jones's Diary
Miss Congeniality
Bring It On
The Notebook
Sweet Home Alabama
Sex and the City
A Walk to Remember

A real galentine is willing
to take sixty-seven practically
identical selfies in order
to get the perfect one.

BESTIES ARE ALWAYS THERE FOR YOU WHEN YOU NEED A HUG. UNLESS YOU'VE JUST LEFT THE GYM. IN WHICH CASE, YOU SHOULD SHOWER FIRST, HUG LATER.

Bestie

Galentines always give your social media posts the love they deserve. And not just because you passive-aggressively asked them if they've seen your new post. Dot dot dot.

BEST FRIENDS ARE ALWAYS
THERE FOR YOU WHEN YOU
NEED THAT EXTRA LITTLE
BOOST OF CONFIDENCE.

If you are bored of doing the same thing every day, take your bestie on a random adventure! Here are some relatively cheap or free ideas to shake up your everyday hang-out routines!

Toy Store

Relive your childhood and take your girlfriend to a toy store! Shoot Nerf guns at each other, bounce on giant balls, ride tricycles that are far too small for you! You might annoy all of the store employees, but you will have a fun time doing so!

Impromptu Fashion Show

Take your galentine to a clothing store, maybe one of your longtime favorites, or maybe a store you would never shop at in a million years for one reason or another. Pick out outfits for each other and have a fashion show in the dressing rooms. If you really want to go big, try this around prom season.

Impromptu Photo Shoot

To start this adventure, let your bestie pick out your outfit, and you pick out hers! Have fun doing hair and makeup, and don't be afraid to try something new! Then find a cool location like a park, a graffiti wall, or the beach and begin your photo shoot! Pose each other and take hilariously awesome snaps! Not only will you have a blast, but you'll always have the photos to remember the day by!

Roller Rink or Laser Tag

Dress up in '80s leg warmers and hit the roller rink, skating to your favorite classic tunes. Or go ninja-style in all black and have a special-ops mission at laser tag. Both of these options are sure to be a hilariously good time.

Karaoke

Whether you go out to a karaoke bar or just plug in an old machine at home, it's always fun to belt out your favorite tunes with your bestie.

Music Video

Do you and your soul sister have a song? If so, choreograph a dance to it and get that shiz on video! You will laugh until your sides ache, and if you decide to upload it, who knows?! Maybe you'll go viral!

New love interests must first pass the bestie test.

BESTIES ARE NEVER
SURPRISED BY YOUR
CHOICE OF OUTFIT. IF
YOU HAVEN'T ALREADY
SENT THEM A PHOTO,
IT'S BECAUSE YOU ARE
WEARING THEIR CLOTHES
AND ARE AFRAID THEY'LL
WANT THEM BACK.

True friendship is knowing that one day I can count on you to hold my wedding dress when I have to pee.

THROWBACK SLUMBER PARTY

You know that moment of pure joy when your favorite '90s jam comes on the radio and you can't help but sing and dance along? Well, why not re-create that feeling for an entire night of throwback fun with your favorite gal pals?! Here are a few tips on how to have a perfect girls' night in, '90s-style.

What to Wear

onesies
matching cartoon pajama sets
anything neon (Fresh Prince, y'all)

What to Serve

Pizza Rolls
Lunchables
Fruit Gushers
Dunkaroos
Fruit by the Foot
Mystic beverages
sugary cereal (or even a cereal bar!)
spiked Capri Sun
Go-Gurt (for the health-conscious)

What to Do

M.A.S.H.

Mad Libs

build a pillow fort

PlayStation or Nintendo competition

piñata (filled with mini bottles!)

truth or dare

hide-and-seek

Bop It and/or Skip-It

Electronic Dream Phone and/or Mall Madness

make bead animals

What to Watch

The Fresh Prince of Bel-Air

Full House and/or *Fuller House*

Saved by the Bell

Family Matters

Step by Step

Dawson's Creek

Beverly Hills, 90210

Felicity

The Wonder Years

Buffy the Vampire Slayer

Sex and the City

Friends

Real galentines know
exactly where they will be
fifty years from now.

BESTIES ARE ALWAYS
THERE TO SUPPORT YOU.
NO MATTER WHAT.

Acknowledgments from Alicia

Writing this book has been an absolutely wonderful (and terrifying) adventure. I am so thankful to St. Martin's Press for giving me this opportunity.

Thank you to my husband, Richard Clancy, for always supporting and believing in me.

I'm beyond grateful to Samantha Farrar for being such a talented artist and for being a great friend. This book would not be what it is without you, your hard work, and your badass illustrations.

Thank you to Sara Goodman and Marc Resnick for their invaluable mentorship throughout this process. And thank you to George Witte and Jen Enderlin for believing in me and this project enough to give it the green light. Also thanks to Laura Clark, who inspired this project, to Anna Gorovoy for her fabulous interior design, to Lauren Friedlander, Sarah Schoot, and Gabi Gantz for their hard work, to Emily Walters for her careful eye, and to everyone else here at SMP who has helped to make this book a reality.

Thank you to my own girl squad for being such positive and supportive influences in my life, especially to my twin sister and other half, Brittany Cox; my mom, Stephanie Adkins; and my older sister, Brandy Sawyer. Also to Madeleine Stallard, Isabelle Fernando, Lauren Jablonski, Jaime Coyne, Katelyn Dykes, Sherrika Mauldin, Christy Tester, Shonna Bernard, Laura Depalma, Christine Cuiule, Molly McGarry, Michelle Quinn, and Danielle Dudek Kaiser. I could name many more friends who have been supportive and wonderful and whom I love dearly, but I'll run out of space on the page.

Thank you to the rest of my family—my dad, Phillip Adkins; my in-laws, Mike, Pat, and James Clancy; my grandparents, Sandra and Joe Murray and Sylvia and Carl Moore; and everyone else. I am sure I'm forgetting many people who deserve my gratitude, so thank you to you as well! I'm very blessed and thankful to have been given this opportunity.

Acknowledgments from Samantha

It has always been a dream of mine to illustrate a book. Not only has that dream come true, but working with a friend has made it even more special. Thank you, Alicia Clancy, for having faith in me and including me in this exciting endeavor. I will be forever grateful for this opportunity as well as your friendship.

Thank you, St. Martin's Press, for taking a chance on an unknown and inexperienced illustrator. I hope I've only made you want to continue taking chances.

I could never thank my husband, Fred Bartz, enough for always supporting me, loving me, and pushing me to do what I love.

Thank you to my family, especially my parents, Melanie and Vince Farrar. You have always lifted me up and given me the confidence to pursue my dreams.

Lastly, I want to thank all the amazing ladies in my life. Your friendships truly mean the world to me.